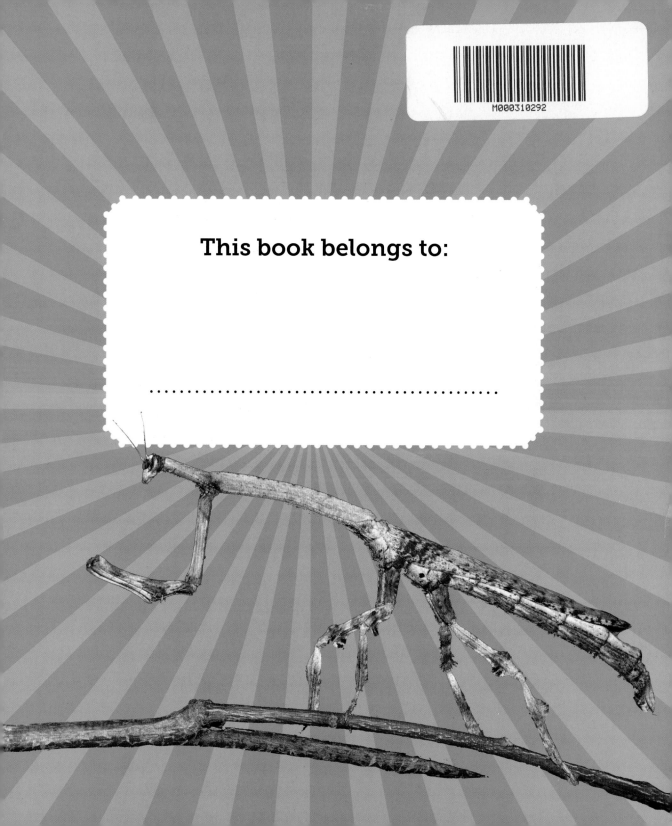

This book belongs to:

....

INCREDIBLE ANIMALS

How this collection works

This collection includes six amazing non-fiction texts that are ideal for encouraging your child's interest in animals, from dangerous predators to household pets! These texts are packed full of fascinating information, with the same high-quality artwork and photos you would expect from any non-fiction book – but they are specially written so that your child can read them for themselves. They are carefully levelled and in line with your child's phonics learning at school.

It's very important for your child to have access to non-fiction as well as stories while they are learning to read. This helps them develop a wider range of reading skills, and prepares them for learning through reading. Most children love finding out about the world as they read – and some children prefer non-fiction to story books, so it's doubly important to make sure that they have opportunities to read both.

How to use this book

Reading should be a shared and enjoyable experience for both you and your child. Pick a time when your child is not distracted by other things, and when they are happy to concentrate for about 15 minutes. Choose just one of the non-fiction texts for each session, so that they don't get too tired. Read the tips on the next page, as they offer ideas and suggestions for getting the most out of this collection.

Tips for reading non-fiction

STEP 1

Before your child begins reading one of the non-fiction texts, look together at the contents page for that particular text. What does your child think the text will be about? Do they know anything about this subject already? Briefly talk about your child's ideas, and remind them of anything they know about the topic if necessary. Look at the page of notes and 'before reading' suggestions for each text, and use these to help introduce the text to your child.

STEP 2

Ask your child to show you some of the non-fiction features in the text – for example, the contents page, glossary and index, photos, labels and fact boxes. Can your child tell you how the contents page and index help you to find your way around the text? Point out that some tricky words are explained in the glossary.

STEP 3

Ask your child to read the text aloud. Encourage them to stop and look at the pictures, and talk about what they are reading either during the reading session, or afterwards. Your child will be able to read most of the words in the text, but if they struggle with a word, remind them to say the sounds in the word from left to right and then blend the sounds together to read the whole word, e.g. *v-a-m-p-ire, vampire*. If they have real difficulty, tell them the word and move on.

STEP 4

When your child has finished reading, talk about what they have found out. Which bits of the text did they like most, and why? Encourage your child to do some of the fun activities that follow each text.

CONTENTS

Perfect Pets

This text looks at the pros and cons of different pets.

Before reading

Talk about pets with your child. Do they have a pet, or do they know anyone who does? What do they think would be good about having a pet? What might they not like about having a pet?

Look out for ...

… a very sleepy pet.

… a pet that can walk upside down.

… a pet that can grow a new leg.

… a pet that has a bath in dust.

PERFECT PETS

CONTENTS

This text will help you pick your perfect pet!

Jill McDougall

Super Dogs

Dogs are great pets because they like to play.

But did you know that dogs have *super* powers?

Dogs can hear sounds that we can't hear. They are super sniffers, too. Dogs can smell at least 1000 times better than people can.

Meet my pet

Amy's dog is called Jazz.
Jazz likes to go to the park with Amy.

Is a dog your perfect pet?

Pros

- ♥ clever
- ♥ loyal

Cons

- ♥ leaves poo to be picked up
- ♥ can be noisy

Cuddly Cats

Cats make cuddly pets and they talk to you, too! A 'meow' can mean 'play with me' or 'stroke me'. A loud meow could mean '*Feed* me'! (Cats can be bossy!)

Cats are sleepy pets. They sleep for about 15 hours every day.

Meet my pet

Luke's cat is called Pixie.
Pixie likes to chase toys.

Is a cat your perfect pet?

Pros	Cons
♥ playful	♠ **sheds** fur
♥ clean	♠ has sharp claws

Clever Geckos

If you don't have much space,
a gecko could be your perfect pet.

Geckos are little lizards.
Most are good climbers.
Their feet stick to walls
to help them climb. They can
even walk upside down!

Molly's gecko is called Tinsel.
Tinsel likes to climb – onto Molly's head!

Is a gecko your perfect pet?

Pros

- ♥ easy to look after
- ♥ quiet

Cons

- ♥ can be shy
- ♥ needs to eat living **prey**

13

Skinny Stick Insects

Stick insects look amazing!
They are long and thin,
just like sticks. Stick insects
are the longest insects.

A stick insect's leg can fall off ...
but sometimes it can grow a
new one!

Meet my pet

Tim's stick insect is called Twiggy. Twiggy likes to walk on Tim's hand.

Is a stick insect your perfect pet?

Pros

♥ quiet
♥ clean

Cons

 has lots of babies (if it's a female!)
♠ can't really play with you

Busy Chickens

Would you like a pet that lives outside? If so, a chicken might be your perfect pet!

Chickens like to be busy. They scratch in the dirt, looking for bugs to eat. Chickens like to have a bath ... in the dust! This is how they look after their feathers.

Meet my pet

Jake's chicken is called Lola. Lola likes to follow Jake around.

Is a chicken your perfect pet?

Pros

- ♥ fun to feed
- ♥ lays eggs

Cons

- ♠ noisy
- ♠ needs space outside

Pick Your Perfect Pet

1. Talk to your family to find out what they think about getting a pet.

2. Find out more about some different pets. You could even look after one for a day.

3. Look at the pros and cons of the pets. Then score each pet with your family.

4. Decide which pet is perfect for you.

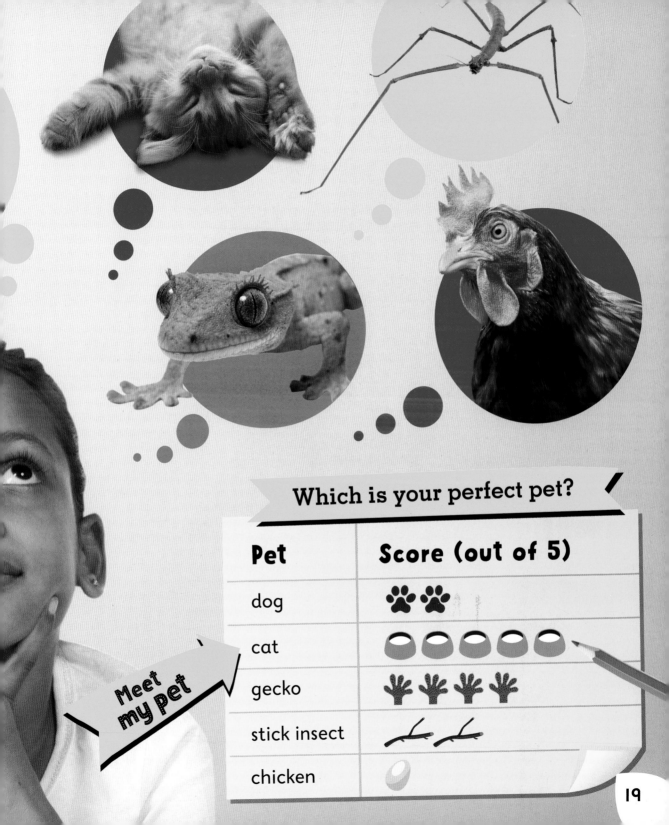

Meet my pet

Which is your perfect pet?

Pet	Score (out of 5)
dog	🐾🐾
cat	🥣🥣🥣🥣🥣
gecko	🌿🌿🌿🌿
stick insect	🌿🌿🌿
chicken	🥚

Glossary

loyal: will always be there for you

prey: an animal that is eaten by another animal

sheds: takes off or drops a covering, such as fur or skin

Index

Talk about it!

Which animal would you most like to have as your pet? Why?

Pets for small spaces

Which are the two best pets to choose if you don't have much space?

21

Deep Down Weird

This text looks at some of the amazing creatures that
live in the deepest parts of the ocean.

Before reading

Look at the contents list and read the weird names of the creatures.
Which creature does your child think sounds the most interesting?
Can they guess what any of these creatures will be like?

Look out for ...

... a fish that can swallow things bigger than itself.

... the snot-flower worm! It has no mouth or stomach ... so how
does it eat?

... a creature that has its own lights.

... a crab that has no eyes.

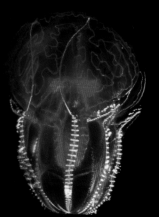

DEEP DOWN WEIRD

CONTENTS

Rob Alcraft

It's Weird Down in the Deep Ocean

Down in the deep ocean there is no sunlight, only darkness. No plants grow. Finding food is hard.

In this weird place, only the weirdest animals can stay alive.

Black Devil Fish

Look at this black devil fish. Its giant mouth is weird but it's useful.

lights up to attract **prey**

The black devil fish can stretch its mouth and **stomach**. It can swallow things bigger than itself.

Vampire Squid

The food is weird down here.

This vampire squid eats **waste**. It rolls its food into slimy balls to eat.

Snot-flower Worm

This is a
snot-flower worm.
It eats the bones of
dead whales but it has
no mouth or stomach.

The snot-flower
worm makes a
hole in the bone.
Then it grows
down into the
bone like a weird
root. Tiny bugs live
in the root of the
snot-flower worm.
They help it to eat.

Loosejaw

It is hard to see in the deep, dark ocean so this weird loosejaw has its own lights.

Lights glow around the loosejaw's eyes, helping it to hunt for food.

light

Sea Cucumber

If this sea cucumber is attacked, bits of its skin tear off. They start glowing.

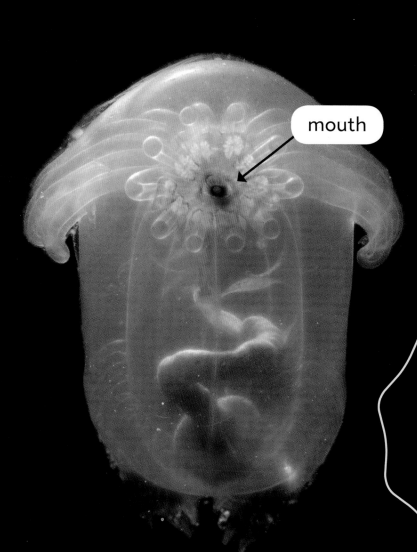

mouth

Then the sea cucumber can slip away safely into the darkness.

Bristle Worm

Without its weird **bristles**, this bristle worm would be cooked alive.

bristles

It lives next to cracks in the **seabed**. Very hot water and gas come out of the cracks. The bristles keep this worm safe.

Yeti Crab

This yeti crab has no eyes.

It finds food by feeling about with its strange, hairy claws.

Goblin Shark

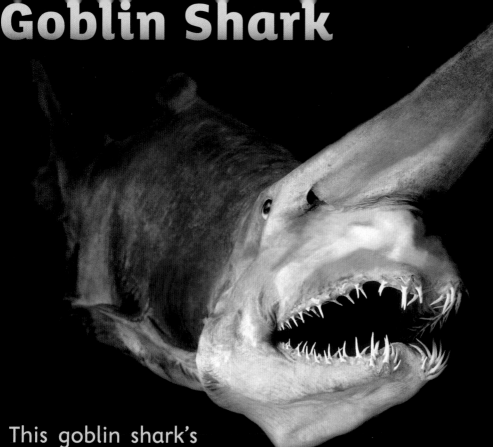

This goblin shark's nose is weird but it's useful. The shark can smell and feel when other animals are nearby. In the darkness, the goblin shark uses its nose to find other animals to eat.

When the goblin shark finds something good to eat, it swallows it whole.

Glass Squid

Looking weird is useful for this glass squid. Its see-through body helps it to hide from animals that might want to eat it.

If it is attacked, it can **swell** up like a football to look scary!

The deep ocean is hard for people to visit and explore, even in a **submarine**. New animals are still being found – like this bloodybelly.

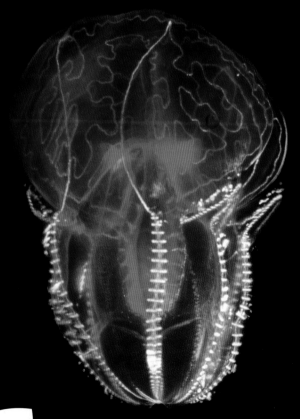

Bloodybelly

Down in the darkness, the bloodybelly glows red. The animals that might want to eat it can't see the colour red, so they can't see the bloodybelly.

Dumbo Octopus

This is a
dumbo octopus.
It can grow as
long as a person.
Only a few
dumbos have
ever been seen.

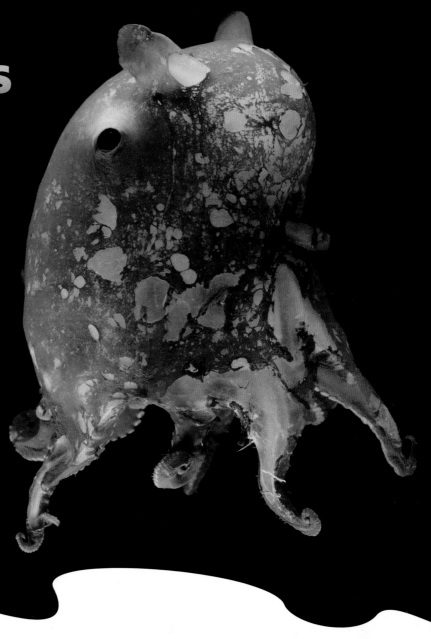

The deep ocean is still a mystery. What other weird
animals might be deep down in the darkness?

Glossary

bristles: hairs that are stiff and short

prey: animals that are hunted and eaten by other animals

seabed: the bottom of the sea

stomach: the part of the body that food goes to

submarine: a vehicle that travels underwater

swell: to get bigger

waste: bits that are left over from living animals and dead animals

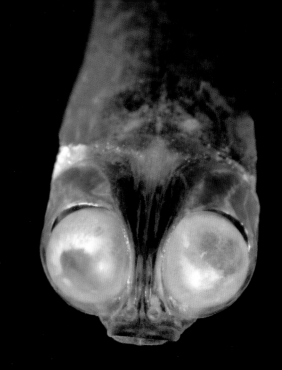

Index

Talk about it!

Which deep sea creature was the most unusual? Why?

Match the creatures

Match the creatures with their names.

vampire squid

snot-flower worm

sea cucumber

goblin shark

Who Eats Who?

This text is all about food chains – it shows how plants and small animals are eaten by bigger animals, all the way up to top predators.

Before reading

Talk with your child about some animals that they know, and what these animals eat. Talk about how some animals eat plants, and some eat other animals.

Look out for ...

... a very big, fierce animal that couldn't survive without grass!

... animals that are herbivores and animals that are carnivores.

... an animal that uses its skin to help it to hunt.

Who EATS Who?

CONTENTS

Teresa Heapy

Food Chains

All living things are part of food chains.
Yes, *all* living things – big and small,
plants and animals!

A food chain is made when one living
thing eats another living thing ...

... and that living thing eats another ... and that living thing eats another.

Yikes!

Yum, dinner time!

frog · eaten by → fox

Why do living things eat each other?

All living things need food. It helps them grow and gives them energy.

Don't Break the Chain!

Every link in a food chain is important. Grass is important to lions, even though they don't eat it.

grass

eaten by

zebra

This food chain starts with grass.

Zebras are **herbivores**. They eat grass. Without grass, zebras wouldn't have anything to eat, and they would die.

Yuck, I don't eat grass! But without grass, there would be no zebras for me to eat!

lion

eaten by

Lions are **carnivores**. They eat zebras. Without zebras and other herbivores, the lions wouldn't have anything to eat either!

All Chained Together

Food chains happen *everywhere*! You'll find them in hot places and in cold places.

Hot places

plant → eaten by → insect

eaten by

snake ← eaten by ← lizard

Snakes are **camouflaged**. Their skin matches their environment, so lizards can't see them coming!

Cold places

shrimp

eaten by

Arctic cod

eaten by

polar bear

eaten by

seal

Polar bears wait for seals near holes in the ice.

45

You're in the Chain, Too!

Humans are in food chains, too. Yes, that means *you!*

Humans are **omnivores** – they can eat plants, fish and meat.

I'd like roast chicken for dinner.

That looks yummy.

corn → eaten by → chicken → eaten by → human

Humans usually buy meat instead of hunting it.

Humans usually cook meat before eating it.

Mmmmm!

Some humans choose not to eat meat. They are called **vegetarians**.

Does the Chain End?

There is a pattern in food chains. A carnivore, such as a lion or a fox, is usually at the top of a food chain. This is because these animals are excellent hunters, or **predators**.

plants **eaten by** deer **ea**

The grizzly bear is a predator. But this food chain does not end with the grizzly bear! No, a food chain never ends!

When a grizzly bear dies, it is eaten by bugs in the ground. They break it down in the soil, and make it into food for the plants ...

Then the chain starts again!

grizzly bear → eaten by → **bugs**

make food for ←

Who Eats Who?

Yes, *all* living things are in food chains –
from lions, to insects, to *you*!

Group 1	eaten by	Group 2	eaten by

Group 1: grass, corn, plants

Group 2: insect, snail, shrimp, Arctic cod, chicken, lizard, frog, deer, seal, zebra

50

Now, take a look back through this text –
and remember ... who eats who?

Group 3 eaten by **Group 4**

grizzly
bear

polar
bear

fox

snake

lion

human

bugs

Glossary

camouflaged: blended in with the background

carnivores: animals that eat meat

herbivores: animals that eat only plants

omnivores: animals and humans that eat both meat and plants

predators: animals that hunt and eat other animals

vegetarians: people who choose not to eat meat

Index

Talk about it!

Are humans carnivores, herbivores or omnivores?

Don't break the chain!

Can you work out the right order for the plants and animals in this food chain?

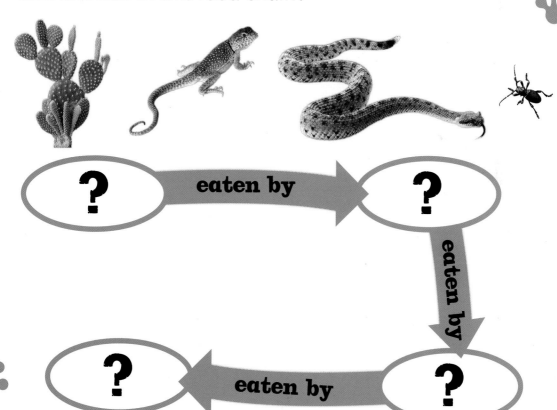

? → **eaten by** → ?

eaten by ↓

? ← **eaten by** ← ?

Colour Codes

This text looks at the different ways that animals and plants use colour – for example, to be seen, to hide, or to warn off an animal that might want to eat them.

Before reading

Can your child think of any really colourful animals? Talk about why animals might be brightly coloured. Do their colours help them to stand out, or to blend into their surroundings?

Look out for ...

… a gecko that is hard to spot because it is camouflaged!

… animals that change colour to match their background.

… animals that change colour because of the food they eat.

… a frog the size of a paper clip!

COLOUR CODES

CONTENTS

Teresa Heapy

Colour in Nature

There are so many colours in <u>nature</u>!

Plants and animals use colours for many different reasons. What are they trying to say? Are they hiding? Or are they showing off?

Colours are used to send many different messages.

to hide

Colour codes
Look out for these codes!

To
Hide

To Be
Seen

to be seen

Food I Eat

! To Warn Off!

To Hunt

Look at Me!

Some plants have very bright colours
so that insects and birds will notice them.

Flowers need bees to carry their **pollen**
to other flowers. They use bright colours
to **attract** the bees.

Most bees like purple and blue flowers best.

pollen

Some plants have bright <u>berries</u>, which contain seeds.
Birds eat the berries and fly away. Later, the seeds come
out in the birds' poo! This helps new plants to grow in
different places.

Some plants grow
red berries so birds can
find them easily.

berries

I'm the Best!

The male peacock uses his colourful tail to attract a female. He spreads it out like a fan and shakes it!

eyespot

The peacock with the most **eyespots** usually attracts the most females.

peacock feather

Male <u>birds of paradise</u> have brightly coloured feathers. They show them off by doing a special dance to attract females.

greater bird of paradise

There are more than 36 different types of birds of paradise.

You Can't See Me
– I'm Hunting!

Some animals, called **predators**, hunt other animals.

Some predators sneak up on their **prey**. They use their colouring to blend in with their surroundings, keeping them hidden.

The tiger's stripes look easy to see here ...

... but in long grass, the stripes make the tiger very hard to see.

The Arctic fox has a white coat that blends in with the snow.

To
Hide

You Can't See Me
– I'm Hiding!

Some animals use colour to hide from predators. This helps keep them safe.

Can you spot this gecko?
Its skin is the same colour as the dead leaves.

This caterpillar uses its colour to blend into the leaf. It's almost invisible!

To Hide

To Hunt

Now You See Me...
Now You Don't!

Some animals can change their skin colour to match the background around them. This helps them hide from predators – and sneak up on their prey!

Cuttlefish change colour to hide from predators such as sharks. Cuttlefish often hunt crabs and small fish.

hiding

Flounder match their skin colour to the sea floor, where they hide from predators.

Flounder wait for shrimp or small fish to swim past – and then they eat them!

Eat a Colour!

Some animals change colour because of the food they eat.

Flamingos have grey feathers when they are born. Their feathers turn pink because of the foods they eat! These foods, such as shrimp and some seaweed, contain a special dye.

adult flamingo

baby flamingo

adult scarlet ibis

baby scarlet ibis

The scarlet ibis is brown when it is young. As it grows, its feathers turn bright red. This happens because the ibis eats shellfish, which contain a red dye.

! To Warn Off!

Watch Out!

Sometimes bright colours mean danger.

The <u>poison dart frog</u> is the size of a paper clip. But even though it's tiny, it doesn't hide from predators. Its bright colour is a warning – its skin is poisonous! If a predator eats the frog, the predator will die.

Poison dart frogs can be lots of different colours.

A <u>coral snake</u>'s bright colours may look beautiful, but they are a warning. Watch out, predators! The coral snake is poisonous.

Colourful Coral

Coral reefs have very clear water. This makes it easy for animals to see and be seen.

In a coral reef, being colourful is the best way to blend in. Some animals are hiding so they can hunt. Others are hiding to stay safe. Some do both!

This coral reef is in the Red Sea, off the coast of Egypt.

Crack the Code

Each of these plants or animals uses their colour for a special reason. Can you match the right code to each one? Look back through the text to see if you are right.

cuttlefish

adult scarlet ibis

tiger

flounder

greater bird of paradise

flower

coral reef

caterpillar

adult flamingo

poison dart frog

berries

Arctic fox

coral snake

gecko

peacock

To Hide

To Be Seen

Food I Eat

! To Warn Off!

To Hunt

75

Glossary

attract: to draw attention

coral reefs: ocean areas filled with coral, where lots of fish and other animals live

eyespots: the patterns on a peacock's feathers, which look a bit like eyes

pollen: a yellow powder that bees carry from flower to flower

predators: animals that hunt other animals

prey: an animal that is hunted by another animal

Index

Talk about it!

Why do I have such a bright red chest?

Word search

Can you find all these colourful creatures?

s	b	d	s	f	l	c	e	u	d
t	e	o	c	l	c	k	g	g	h
p	e	a	c	o	c	k	k	e	e
c	n	r	c	u	r	m	i	l	f
f	r	o	g	n	t	i	g	e	r
m	i	b	y	d	d	b	e	f	s
f	v	i	r	e	s	i	c	y	s
e	r	k	h	r	i	s	k	u	i
f	l	a	m	i	n	g	o	h	d

bee

peacock

tiger

gecko

flounder

flamingo

ibis

frog

Bug Buzz!

This text is full of fun facts and information about amazing insects, from house flies, to ancient dragonflies the size of a duck!

Before reading

Ask your child what they already know about insects. How many different types can they name? Look at the contents list to find out what kind of information is in the text

---

Look out for ...

... a flower seen through the eyes of a bee!

... an enormous dragonfly.

... an insect that lives in your home.

... a caterpillar that pulls a face at predators.

BUG BUZZ!

CONTENTS

Wayne Gerdtz

FIND AN INSECT

Insects are everywhere – there are more insects than any other type of animal on Earth!

Some insects crawl or jump. Some insects fly.

All insects have:

one pair of antennae

a body that has three parts

six legs

a hard outer shell,
called an exoskeleton

If you find an animal
with all these body parts,

you have found
an insect!

INSECTS FROM LONG AGO

Insects have lived on Earth for a long time. Many insects were around even before the dinosaurs!

This insect **fossil** is more than 40 million years old!

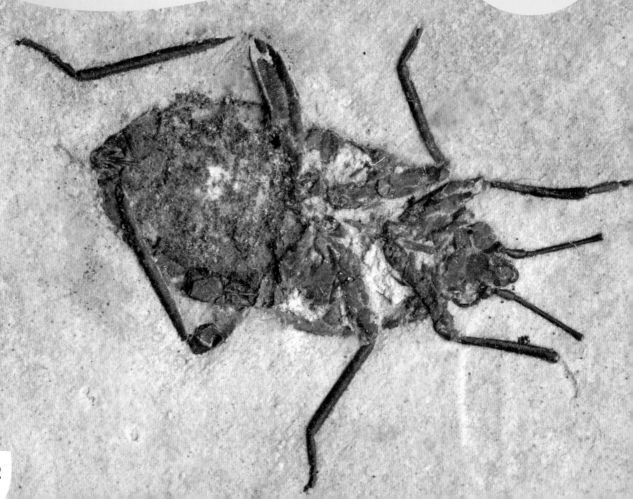

Millions of years ago, forests buzzed with insects. Some of them were *enormous*. Imagine a dragonfly as big as a duck!

INSECT HOMES

Insects live in many different places. Just like humans, they build their homes in places where they can find food.

lakes and rivers

hot deserts

snow-topped mountains

your home

rainforests

In rainforests, scientists think there are millions of types of insects that nobody has ever seen!

BABY INSECTS

All baby insects hatch from eggs.

Some baby insects look like little adult insects, such as these baby cockroaches.

Other baby insects look completely different from the adults. They go through big changes as they grow up.

baby cockroach

1 A butterfly starts life as a caterpillar in a small egg.

2 The caterpillar hatches from the egg … and it eats and eats.

adult cockroach

4 ... into a butterfly.

3 The caterpillar becomes a **chrysalis** (*say kris-a-lis*) and starts changing ...

SPECIAL EYES

Many insects have special eyes called compound eyes. Compound eyes are made up of many tiny parts – these are like lots of mini eyes.

Some insects have compound eyes that help them look at different things all at once. This means that insects can find food *and* look out for danger at the same time!

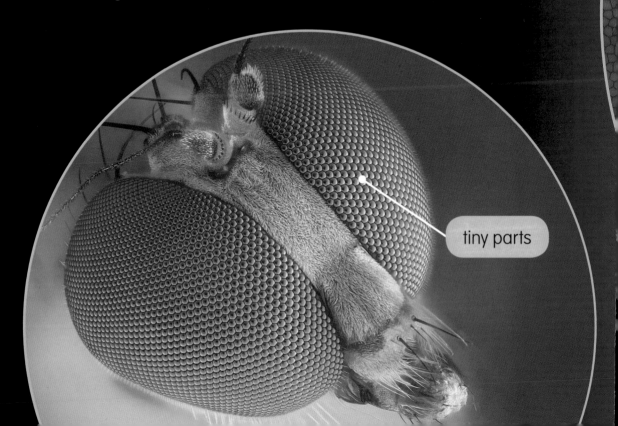

tiny parts

A flower looks very different through the eyes of a bee!

Each tiny part of an insect's eye sees something different!

AMAZING MOUTHS

Insects don't have teeth! Instead, their mouths have special parts to help them eat. Each type of insect has different parts in its mouth, depending on the food it eats.

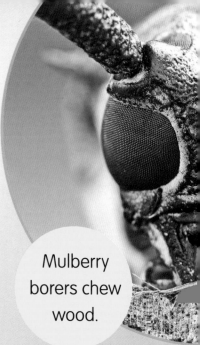

Mulberry borers chew wood.

Some insects have mouths that bite and chew.

Shield bugs suck juices from plants.

Some have mouths that stab and suck.

Other insects have mouths that soak up food, just like a sponge!

Houseflies soak up their food.

WONDERFUL WINGS

Insects were the first flying animals on Earth. Most insects have four wings. Other insects, such as flies, only have two wings.

A dragonfly's wings are so thin that they are see-through.

Dragonflies have four long wings. This means they can fly very fast.

The patterns on this butterfly's wings warn predators that it tastes bad!

Butterflies have beautiful patterns on their wings. Sometimes these patterns help to protect the butterfly from **predators**. The patterns also help to **attract** other butterflies.

SIX SUPER LEGS

Insects have six legs and each leg has six main parts. Insects use their legs to do different jobs such as burrowing, catching food, jumping and swimming.

Mole crickets use their strong front legs to dig.

The praying mantis has legs like hooks to hold its food.

Grasshoppers use their long legs to jump away from predators.

Backswimmers have legs like paddles so they can swim across the water on their backs.

If a young stick insect loses a leg, it can grow a new one!

WEIRD AND WONDERFUL

There are lots of weird and wonderful insects all around the world.

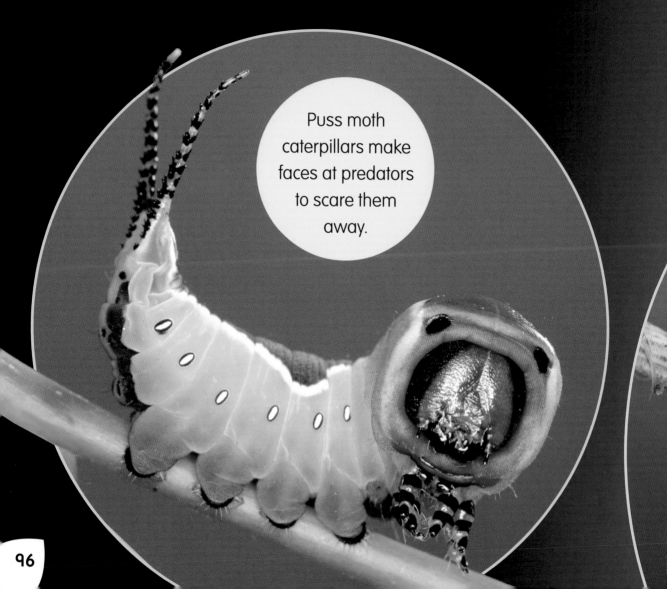

Puss moth caterpillars make faces at predators to scare them away.

Treehoppers use their long, spiky horns to scare away predators.

The gladiator insect gets its name from its exoskeleton, which looks like **armour**.

WE NEED INSECTS

Even though some insects bite or sting, insects can also be very helpful.

Insects such as bees, wasps and butterflies move pollen from flower to flower. This helps plants to grow new fruit and seeds for us to eat.

Baby insects, such as grubs, eat our food scraps.

This grub is eating a piece of old fruit.

Some insects make food that people like to eat — honey is made by bees!

Some insects, such as ladybirds, eat pests that damage our plants.

So next time you tell an insect to buzz off, remember: *we need insects!*

GLOSSARY

armour: a tough outer layer to protect a soft body, such as metal armour worn in battle

attract: to draw attention

chrysalis: the hard outer shell on a moth or butterfly in the stage before it becomes an adult with wings

fossil: the hard remains of an animal or plant that lived millions of years ago

predators: animals that hunt and eat other animals

INDEX

Talk about it!

Can you remember my name? Why am I special?

Which bug am I?

Read the clues to find out which animals are being described.

1. I am spotty and I eat pests.
2. I can swim across the water on my back.
3. If I lose a leg, I can grow a new one.
4. You can see through my wings.
5. I suck up my food.
6. I turn into a butterfly.

Answers: 1. ladybird; 2. backswimmer; 3. stick insect; 4. dragonfly; 5. house fly; 6. caterpillar

Our Class Tiger

This text describes how some children sponsor a tiger cub. They learn about why tigers are endangered and they watch the tiger grow up until it is old enough to be released into the wild.

Before reading

Talk about tigers and share anything your child already knows about them. Explain that in this text, children decide to sponsor a tiger cub, and they find out lots about it.

Look out for ...

… the meaning of the name Berhargo.

… the Indonesian word for tiger.

… the distance a tiger can jump.

… tiger food! What do tigers eat?

OUR CLASS TIGER

CONTENTS

Aleesah Darlison

Our Class Tiger

Hi, my name is Rose Carter and I'm in class 3M.

This year we are doing a special class project. We're sponsoring an **endangered** animal. The animal is a tiger!

tail

stripes

whiskers

webbed paws

Today there are fewer than 3200 tigers living in the wild. Scientists believe that in 30 years, there might be no tigers left.

Sumatran Tigers

The tiger we're sponsoring lives on an island called Sumatra (*say soo-mar-tra*). That's in a country called Indonesia (*say In-don-ee-zia*).

Even though we don't live there, we can still help the Sumatran tigers.

Sumatra

INDONESIA

**SPONSOR
A TIGER!**

Tigers are endangered because they are hunted for their skins, meat and body parts. This is **illegal**.

At weekends and after school, we do lots of jobs to earn money. Then each month, we send the money to **WWF** (The World Wide Fund for Nature). The money is used to look after our tiger.

Our Tiger Cub

Our class has sponsored a tiger cub called Berharga (*say* Ber-har-ga), which means 'precious' in Indonesian. He lives in a **sanctuary** and a man named Darma looks after him.

A tiger mother usually gives birth to three cubs at a time. But sometimes she can have as many as seven cubs at a time!

In the wild, tigers live for about ten years.

Sponsoring a Tiger

When we first sponsored Berharga, we were sent a toy tiger in a gift box. Our teacher, Mr Morrison, keeps the toy on a special spot on his desk. Every weekend, someone in our class takes toy Berharga home.

Tigers have stripes on their skin as well as striped fur.

We also got a sponsorship **certificate**, a tiger fact sheet and a photo of Berharga.

Berharga, the Sumatran tiger

TIGER FACTS

🐾 Tigers are the biggest species in the cat family and they are very rare.

🐾 Tigers have lived in Sumatra for over a million years.

🐾 The Indonesian word for tiger is 'harimau' (say har-eem-ow).

🐾 A female tiger is called a tigress.

🐾 A tiger can jump a distance of 10 metres.

Baby Berharga

Berharga was five months old when he was rescued. He still needed to drink milk!

Berharga's mother had been shot by hunters.

Tigers live in forests. Sometimes forests are cut down to make way for palm-oil farms. Palm oil is used in a lot of soap and food.

SAY "NO!"
TO PRODUCT
THAT USE
PALM OIL.

Cubs at Play

When Berharga was seven months old, he loved playing with other tiger cubs. They might look like they're just having fun but they're learning and growing stronger, too.

Playing helps tiger cubs learn how to chase, jump and climb.

Tiger cubs are born with their eyes sealed shut, so they can't see. Their eyes open when they are between six and twelve days old.

Tiger Food

By the time Berharga was ten months old, he had grown so much! He didn't drink milk any more. Instead, he was fed a special diet of meat and was taught to hunt.

TIGERS EAT:

gibbon

water buffalo

deer

Tigers are **carnivores.**

Tigers usually have 30 teeth.

117

Berharga Goes Swimming

Berharga had his first birthday. He went swimming at the sanctuary.

Tigers are good swimmers. It gets very hot in Sumatra so tigers go swimming to keep cool.

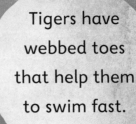

Tigers have webbed toes that help them to swim fast.

Berharga is eating a piece of meat while he swims.

Tigers can swim up to six kilometres at a time.

119

Berharga Grows Up

When Berharga was one year and seven months old, Darma wrote to say that soon Berharga would be too big to stay at the sanctuary. He needed to move to a national park, where he could have his own space but still be safe.

Our class wrote goodbye letters to Berharga and made thank-you cards for Darma.

Goodbye Berharga

THANK YOU DARMA

Tigers become **independent** when they are about two years old.

Tigers are **nocturnal**. They can see six times better than humans at night.

121

Saying Goodbye

When we got our final photo of Berharga, everyone was excited for him but sad to say goodbye.

This is the end of our project but we must not stop helping the tigers. Anything people can do, no matter how small, can make a difference. Will you help them, too?

STAY SAFE, BERHARGA. WE WILL NEVER FORGET YOU!

To sponsor your own tiger or another endangered animal, visit www.wwf.org

123

Glossary

carnivores: animals that eat meat

certificate: a piece of paper showing that something has happened

endangered: when a type of animal may soon not exist anymore

illegal: against the law

independent: able to care for yourself

nocturnal: asleep during the day and active at night

sanctuary: a protected place where people take care of sick and injured wildlife

WWF: an organisation that helps protect animals and the environment (also known as the World Wide Fund for Nature)

Index

Talk about it!

What kind of animal would you like to sponsor? Why?

Unscramble the labels

Unscramble the words to label the different parts of the tiger.

i s er s wh k

s s r e p i t

s aw p

ai t l

OXFORD
UNIVERSITY PRESS

Great Clarendon Street, Oxford, OX2 6DP, United Kingdom

Oxford University Press is a department of the University of Oxford. It furthers the University's objective of excellence in research, scholarship, and education by publishing worldwide. Oxford is a registered trade mark of Oxford University Press in the UK and in certain other countries

Perfect Pets text © Jill McDougall 2014
Illustrations by Helen Dardik

Deep Down Weird text © Rob Alcraft 2014

Who Eats Who? text © Teresa Heapy 2014
Illustrations by Rebecca Elliott

Colour Codes text © Teresa Heapy 2014

Bug Buzz! text © Wayne Gerdtz 2014
Illustrations by Cat McInnes

Our Class Tiger text © Aleesah Darlison 2014
Illustrations by Antonia Stylianou

The moral rights of the authors has been asserted

This Edition published in 2019

British Library Cataloguing in Publication Data
Data available

ISBN: 978-0-19- 276970-1

10 9 8 7 6 5 4 3 2 1

Paper used in the production of this book is a natural, recyclable product made from wood grown in sustainable forests. The manufacturing process conforms to the environmental regulations of the country of origin.

Printed in China

Acknowledgements

Series Editor: Nikki Gamble

Perfect Pets

Designed and typeset by Ana Cosma

The publisher would like to thank the following for permission to reproduce photographs: **p6:** Ace Stock Limited/Alamy; **p8/9:** Emery Way/Getty Images; **p9:** Ron Levine/Getty Images; **p10** and **p11:** Vita Khorzhevska/Shutterstock; **p11:** Odilon Dimier/PhotoAlto/Getty Images; **p12** and **p13:** Michiel de Wit/Shutterstock; **p13:** Ace Stock Limited/Alamy; **p14** and **p15:** Zadiraka Evgenii/Shutterstock; **p15:** Noel Hendrickson/Masterfile; **p16** and **p17:** Anthony Lee/Getty Images; **p17:** Stephen Simpson/Getty Images; **p18** and **p19:** Michael Jung/Shutterstock; **p18:** Emery Way/Getty Images; **p19:** Nattika/Shutterstock; Vita Khorzhevska/Shutterstock; Michiel de Wit/Shutterstock; Zadiraka Evgenii/Shutterstock; Anthony Lee/Getty Images

Deep Down Weird

The publisher would like to thank the following for permission to produce photographs: **p23:** Deep-Sea Photography; **p24:** SeaPics.com/Solvin; **p25:** SeaPics.com/Doug; **p26:** Vampyroteuthis infernalis © 2004 MBARI; **p27:** © The Trustees of the Natural History Museum, London; **p28:** Imagequestmarine/PJH; **p29:** Photo by Larry Madin © Woods Hole Oceanographic Institution; **p30:** SeaPics.com/Susan Dabritz; **p31:** © Ifremer/A. Fifis, The Ifremer Institute. Courtesy M. Segonzac (MNHN); **p32:** SeaPics.com/David; **p33:** Imagequestmarine/Peter Batson; (b) Deep-Sea Photography; **p34:** Lampocteis cruentiventer © MBARI; **p35:** Davis Shale/naturepl.com; **p36:** Dante Fenolio/SCIENCE PHOTO LIBRARY

Who Eats Who?

Designed and typeset by Fiona Lee, Pounce Creative

The publisher would like to thank the following for permission to reproduce photographs: **p41:** Jonathan Barnes/Getty Images; **p42:** Gayvoronskaya_Yana/Shutterstock; **p42** and **p43:** WitthayaP/Shutterstock; **p43:** Barcroft Media/Getty Images; **p44:** fivespots/Shutterstock; mlorenzphotography/Getty Images; ithinksky/Istockphoto; Alex Wild/Visuals Unlimited/ Corbis; **p45:** Ken Canning/Getty Images; Alaska Stock/ Alamy; David Shale/Nature Picture Library; Viada Z/Shutterstock; **p46:** Marko Tomicic/ Shutterstock; PhotoAlto sas/Alamy; Lena Pan/Shutterstock; grocap/Shutterstock;

Colour Codes

Designed and typeset by Ana Cosma

The publisher would like to thank the following for permission to reproduce photographs: **p55, p70** and **p75:** Dirk Ercken/Alamy; **p56:** Getty Images/Barcroft Media; **p56** and **p57:** Switch32/amanaimagesRF/Getty Images; **p57:** Wayne Lynch/All Canada Photos/Corbis; **p58** and **p74:** Willi Schmitz/Getty Images; **p59** and **p74:** WILDLIFE GmbH/Alamy; **p60** and **p74:** F1online digitale Bildagentur GmbH/Alamy; **p60** and **p75:** Evgeniya Moroz/Shutterstock; **p61:** Alcibbum Photography/Corbis; **p62** and **p74:** Carol Yepes/Getty Images; **p63:** Steve Winter/Getty Images; **p63** and **p75:** Alaska Stock/Corbis; **p64** and **p75:** Thomas Marent/Minden Pictures/Corbis; **p65** and **p75:** Jasenka Luksa/Shutterstock; **p66** and **p74:** Gary Bell/OceanwideImages.com; **p66:** Image ID: 0128420-NMA. Copyright © Nigel Marsh/SeaPics.com; **p67** and **p74:** Beth Swanson/Shutterstock; **p68** and **p75:** Anup Shah/Corbis; **p69:** Alucard2100/Shutterstock; **p70:** Adam Jones/Visuals Unlimited/Corbis; **p71** and **p75:** Getty Images/Mark Kostich; **p72** and **p75:** Gary Bell/OceanwideImages.com; **p76:** MPanchenko/Shutterstock;

Bug Buzz!

Designed and typeset by Cristina Neri, Canary Graphic Design

The publisher would like to thank the following for permission to reproduce photographs: **p79:** Ian McKinnell/Getty Images; **p80** and **p81** background: Hiroshi Higuchi/Getty Images; **p80:** Stephen Dalton/Minden Pictures/Corbis; Roland Bogush/Getty Images; **p81:** Peter Waters/Shutterstock; **p82:** Ed Reschke/Getty Images; **p83:** Walter Myers/Science Photo Library; **p84:** Danita Delimont/Getty Images; Ian McKinnell/ Getty Images; **p85:** TeguhSantosa/Getty Images; Jan Stromme/Getty Images; Minden Pictures/Masterfile; **p86:** Papilio/Alamy; **p86:** Marvin Dembinsky Photo Associates/Alamy; **p87:** Don Johnston/Alamy; **p87:** Thomas Kitchin & Victoria Hurst/First Light/Corbis; **p87:** Sinclair Stammers/Science Photo Library; **p87** and **p99:** Rechtsanwalt/Shutterstock; **p88:** lauriek/Getty Images; **p89:** Fuse/Getty Images; **p90:** Berndt Fischer/Getty Images; **p90** and **p91:** Narinbg/Shutterstock; **p91:** F1online digitale Bildagentur GmbH/Alamy; **p92:** Cisca Castelijns/Foto Natura/Minden Pictures/Corbis; **p93:** Leena Robinson/Shutterstock; **p94** and **p95:** Scott Camazine/Alamy; **p94:** blickwinkel/Alamy; **p95:** Stephen Dalton/Minden Pictures/Corbis; **p95:** Michael Durham/Minden Pictures/Corbis; **p96:** Ingo Arndt/Nature Picture Library; **p97:** Piotr Naskrecki/Minden Pictures/ FLPA; karthik photography/Getty Images; **p98:** Rolf Nussbaumer Photography/Alamy; **p98:** blickwinkel/Alamy; **p99:** Graphic Science/Alamy; StudioSmart/Shutterstock

Our Class Tiger

The publisher would like to thank the following for permission to reproduce photographs: **p103:** CRG Photo/Alamy; **p104:** Lindsay Edwards; **p105:** Tambako The Jaguar/Flickr; **p107:** Lindsay Edwards; **p107:** tbkmedia.de/Alamy; **p108:** Lindsay Edwards; **p109:** Getty Images; **p110** (toy): Yykkaa/Dreamstime.com; **p110:** Lindsay Edwards; **p110** and **p111:** Dreamworld, Patrick Martin-Vegue/AAP Image; **p111:** and inside back cover: Bernhard Richter/Dreamstime.com; **p112:** Skynesher/istockphoto; Auscape/UIG/Getty Images; **p113:** Darren Whiteside/Reuters; **p114:** Nicolesy/istockphoto; **p114** and **p115:** Joel Sartore/Getty Images; **p115:** AAP Photo/Binsar Bakkara; **p116:** Vikram Raghuvanshi/istockphoto; **p117:** John Carnemolla/Shutterstock; Kevin Sawford/Alamy; **p118:** Johnny Greig/istockphoto; **p118** and **p119:** Memorix Photography/Shutterstock; **p120:** Lindsay Edwards; **p121:** Rafael Ben-Ari/Alamy; **p122:** Lindsay Edwards; **p122:** Momentimages/Getty Images; **p122** and **p123:** Tom Brakefield/Getty Images; **p124:** Bernhard Richter/Dreamstime.com **Background images** by Photo-master/Shutterstock; Bplanet/Shutterstock; Flas100/Shutterstock; d13/Shutterstock; Tomas Jasinskis/Shutterstock; Nik Merkulov/Shutterstock; Vector illustration/Shutterstock; R-studio/Shutterstock; Tratong/Shutterstock; Arigato/Shutterstock; Barbaliss/Shutterstock; Marko Poplasen/Shutterstock; Furtseff/Shutterstock

All other images Shutterstock

Cover images Shutterstock